EXPLORING OUR OCEANS

MAKO SHARKS

▲ SUSAN H. GRAY

Published in the United States of America by Cherry Lake Publishing
Ann Arbor, Michigan
www.cherrylakepublishing.com

Consultants: Dominique A. Didier, PhD, Associate Professor, Department of Biology, Millersville University;
Marla Conn, ReadAbility, Inc.
Editorial direction: Red Line Editorial
Book design and illustration: Sleeping Bear Press

Photo Credits: iStockphoto/Thinkstock, cover, 1, 23; Bryan Toro/iStockphoto, 5; Sleeping Bear Press, 6;
SeaPics.com, 9, 15, 21; Dorling Kindersley RF/Thinkstock, 11; Dorling Kindersley, 13; Shutterstock
Images, 16, 27; Matt Jones/Shutterstock, 18; David Olah/iStockphoto, 25; Brad Dyksen/iStockphoto, 28

Library of Congress Cataloging-in-Publication Data

Gray, Susan Heinrichs.
  Mako sharks / Susan H. Gray.
     p. cm. — (Exploring our oceans)
Audience: 008.
Audience: Grades 4 to 6.
Includes index.
ISBN 978-1-62431-409-4 (hardcover) — ISBN 978-1-62431-485-8 (pbk.) — ISBN 978-1-62431-447-6 (pdf)
— ISBN 978-1-62431-523-7 (ebook)
1. Mako sharks—Juvenile literature. I. Title.

QL638.95.L3G72 2014
597.3'3—dc23   2013006183

Cherry Lake Publishing would like to acknowledge the work of
The Partnership for 21st Century Skills. Please visit www.p21.org
for more information.

Printed in the United States of America
Corporate Graphics Inc.
July 2013
CLFA11

ABOUT THE AUTHOR

Susan H. Gray has a master's degree in zoology. She enjoys writing about science and animals.
Susan and her husband, Michael, live in Cabot, Arkansas, with their many pets.

TABLE OF CONTENTS

CHAPTER 1
Where Makos Live 4

CHAPTER 2
Built for Speed 8

CHAPTER 3
Chomp! Chomp! 14

CHAPTER 4
Pups and Adults 20

CHAPTER 5
Threats 24

THINK ABOUT IT 30
LEARN MORE 31
GLOSSARY 32
INDEX 32

WHERE MAKOS LIVE

The mako shark swam slowly and quietly in the ocean. Suddenly, something swished past the shark. The object was blue and silver, and it was huge. The mako shot after it. It was a big, tasty swordfish.

The swordfish was fast, but the shark was faster. Soon the mako was upon it and snapped at the swordfish's tail. The swordfish turned in a flash. It thrashed its sharp beak back and forth. Its beak caught the shark in the side, and the shark jerked away. The swordfish saw its chance to escape and sped off.

[21ST CENTURY SKILLS LIBRARY]

Mako sharks swim near the surface of the ocean and at great depths.

LOOK AGAIN

LOOK AT THIS MAKO'S BODY. WHAT FEATURES MAKE IT A GOOD PREDATOR?

RANGE MAP

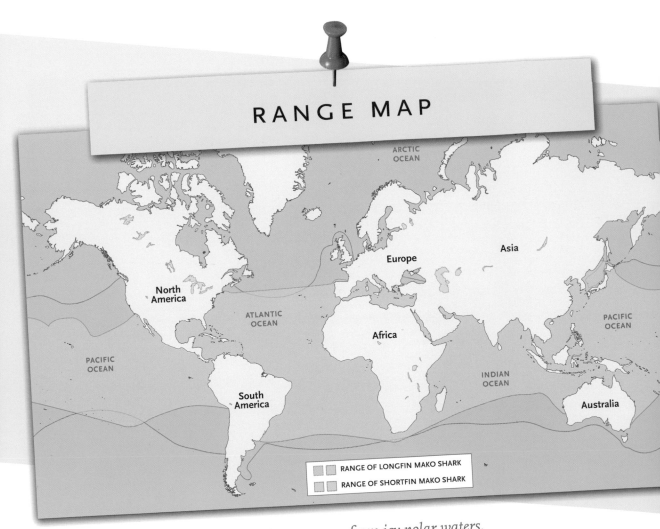

ARCTIC OCEAN

North America

Europe

Asia

ATLANTIC OCEAN

PACIFIC OCEAN

Africa

PACIFIC OCEAN

South America

INDIAN OCEAN

Australia

RANGE OF LONGFIN MAKO SHARK
RANGE OF SHORTFIN MAKO SHARK

Mako sharks stay away from icy polar waters.

Mako sharks usually have better luck. These predators are so fast and fierce they usually catch their prey. They easily chase down fish and other animals in the ocean.

Mako sharks live alone in warm and **temperate** seas around the world. They are found in the Atlantic, Pacific, and Indian Oceans. They seldom go into the icy polar waters.

They often swim to great depths. Mako sharks can dive to 2,400 feet (732 m) and more. This shows they can stand cold water at great pressure.

Makos swim the open ocean and along coastlines. People have seen them off the coasts of the United States and Mexico. The sharks have also been spotted near Cuba, Brazil, Spain, South Africa, Australia, and Japan. ◢

CHAPTER 2

BUILT FOR SPEED

Mako sharks are built for swimming fast and chasing prey. Their bodies are long and streamlined. They are thickest at the center and narrow at the ends. This shape helps them slice through the water at very high speeds. Makos are among the fastest sharks in the ocean. Swimming at 20 miles per hour (32 kmph) is no problem for them.

Like all sharks, makos do not have bones. Instead, they have skeletons made of **cartilage**. Cartilage is a tough, strong material. It is flexible and lighter than bone. This skeleton helps keep the shark from sinking. It also helps the fish make tight turns.

The mako shark is a fierce ocean predator.

The shark's fins aid in swimming, steering, and braking. Fins also help keep the body upright. The largest fins are the pectoral, first dorsal, and tail fins. Pectoral fins are on the shark's sides just behind the head. The first dorsal fin rises straight up from the shark's back. The tail fin is large and stiff. The shark swishes it back and forth to propel itself through the water.

A mako has a pointed snout and large eyes. Its huge mouth is filled with about 50 razor-sharp teeth. Five gill slits are on each side of the head. The shark's gills are just inside the slits.

The gills are delicate structures loaded with blood vessels. As the shark swims, water passes over the gills. Oxygen in the water is drawn into the blood vessels of the gills. Blood then carries the oxygen throughout the animal's body. The muscles need lots of oxygen in order for the mako to swim quickly.

There are two types of mako sharks: shortfin makos and longfin makos. Shortfins have pectoral fins that are

BODY DIAGRAM

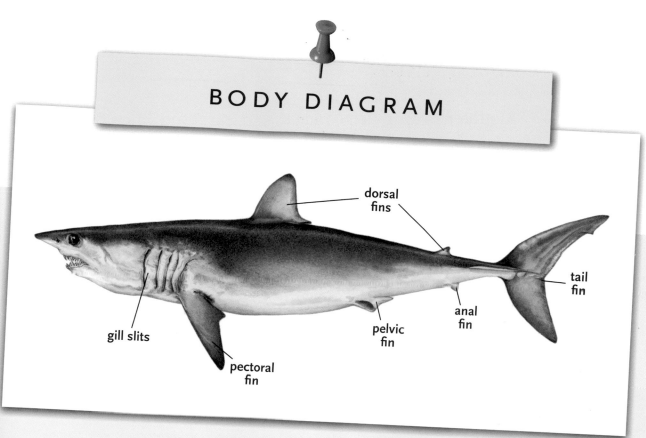

dorsal
fins

tail
fin

anal
fin

pelvic
fin

gill slits

pectoral
fin

The mako shark's body is built for fast swimming.

shorter than their heads. The pectoral fins of longfins are as long as, or longer than, the heads.

The two kinds of makos have very similar colors. Shortfins are metallic blue on top. Their undersides are white. Longfins are blue-gray or dark gray on their backs, sides, snouts, and chins. Their bellies are white. This coloring is called **countershading**.

Countershading helps hide the sharks, even when they are out in the open ocean. Imagine that a prey animal is swimming above the shark. When that animal looks down, it looks into deeper, darker water. The dark back of the mako blends into the darkness, so the shark is less visible. The prey animal might not see the predator. Another prey animal swimming beneath the shark might experience something similar. When it looks up, it peers into water lit by the sun. The white belly of the mako blends into the light.

Both types of makos live in warm and temperate areas around the world. Scientists know more about shortfins though. This is because shortfins are more commonly seen. They are caught by fishing crews more often. People sometimes spot shortfins along coastlines. Scientists believe longfins swim at greater depths. Fishing crews are less likely to catch them. Fewer people see them.

When people do catch makos, it often makes the news. Everyone is amazed to see how huge these sharks can be. Shortfins reach about 12.5 feet (3.8 m) in length. Longfins

The longfin mako is a bit darker than the shortfin mako.

LOOK AGAIN

LOOK AT THIS ILLUSTRATION OF A LONGFIN MAKO. WHY DO YOU THINK IT IS DARKER THAN THE SHORTFIN MAKO?

stretch almost 14 feet (4.3 m). The biggest makos weigh well over 1,000 pounds (454 kg). This is more than the weight of about 15 fourth graders! ◣

CHAPTER 3

CHOMP! CHOMP!

Mako sharks swim in open waters. They eat other animals that swim in open waters too. Makos eat mostly mackerel, tunas, swordfish, bluefish, anchovies, herring, cod, and squid. Sometimes they also feed on dolphins, sea turtles, and other sharks. Some scientists say makos need about 4.4 pounds (2 kg) of food each day. This is about the same weight as a large chicken.

Makos are such fast swimmers few animals can escape them. Their biggest problem might be with swordfish or other sharks that fight back. But even then,

Makos have razor-sharp teeth.

Swordfish can be challenging prey for makos.

LOOK AGAIN

TAKE A CLOSER LOOK AT THIS SWORDFISH. WHAT CHARACTERISTICS MIGHT HELP IT FIGHT OFF A MAKO SHARK?

makos have a great weapon—their teeth. Some of their teeth curve inward. They lock into the flesh of prey. The curved teeth keep the fighting prey from pulling away.

Most sharks are fully **cold-blooded**. This means the sharks' body temperatures stay about the same as the temperature of their environment. In very cold water, their bodies cool down. The sharks move slowly and cannot react quickly. When they move into temperate water, their muscles warm up. The sharks can swim faster, and they are more alert. They can chase their prey more easily.

Only a few sharks are able to keep their body temperature warmer than the surrounding water. The heat in their blood is kept in their bodies. This helps keep them warm even in cooler waters. Sharks that have this ability are considered partially **warm-blooded**. Mako sharks are partially warm-blooded. Their unusual circulatory systems are what allow them to swim so fast, even in cold water.

A mako shark bites the catch of a fisherman.

A mako can keep certain body parts extra warm. When the shark swims, its muscles warm up. They produce heat. Blood flowing through the muscles also heats up. Fresh blood coming into the muscles is a little cooler. Before reaching the muscles, this cooler blood passes through a tight wad of tiny blood vessels. There, vessels carrying warm blood are all tangled up with the vessels carrying cooler blood. While passing through this wad, the cooler blood warms up. So the fresh blood is already heated by the time it reaches the muscles. Muscle activity heats it up even more. The mako is like an athlete who has warmed up. The super-heated shark is ready to zoom after its prey.

Only makos and a few other sharks have these little wads of blood vessels. They keep the sharks' swimming muscles extra warm. They allow the sharks to swim in deep, cold waters. They help the sharks react quickly. ◢

PUPS AND ADULTS

It takes years before mako sharks are old enough to **mate** and have babies. Males are old enough to mate when they are around seven to nine years old. Females, however, do not have babies until they are in their late teens.

When makos mate, some of the female's eggs are fertilized. The fertilized eggs develop shells of thin tissue. Soon, the tissue falls away and the baby sharks inside are revealed.

[21ST CENTURY SKILLS LIBRARY]

Mako females are older than males when they first mate.

At this time, the baby makos each have a bulging belly full of yolk. The yolk provides food for the growing sharks. As the yolk disappears, the baby makos need a new food supply. The mother releases more eggs, and the babies eat them.

It takes about 15 to 18 months for the babies to develop. By this time, the babies are quite crowded. Longfin mothers carry two to eight large babies at a time. Shortfins generally give birth to eight to ten smaller **pups**.

Mother sharks look for special, safe places to have their pups. These places are called nurseries. Experts think the Mediterranean Sea, the southern California coast, and spots near Portugal are mako nurseries. At birth, shortfin pups are about 24 to 28 inches (61–71 cm) long. Longfin pups are about 38 to 47 inches (97–119 cm) in length. This is longer than a baseball bat. Each pup looks almost identical to its mother, only smaller. As soon as the pups are born, they are on their own. Mother makos do not take care of their pups at all.

Mako pups grow into large, powerful adults.

In its first year, a mako pup grows at an amazing rate. Before its first birthday, the shark can grow as much as 24 inches (61 cm) in length. Growth slows down as the shark gets older. By the time female makos are ready to have babies of their own, they are very large. Adult females can weigh more than 500 pounds (227 kg). ◢

GO DEEPER

WHAT IS THE MAIN IDEA OF THIS PARAGRAPH? PROVIDE ONE POINT THAT SUPPORTS THIS.

THREATS

A mako is an **apex** predator. This means it eats other animals, but nothing eats it. For young makos, this isn't quite the case. They sometimes do become prey for other sharks. They are too small to win a fight. They are not fast enough to escape bigger predators.

Makos have other threats. They have to deal with **parasites**. Tiny animals called copepods latch on to the sharks. They prefer soft places such as the shark's gums or gills. The copepods burrow into the tissue and lock themselves down. They shove their tube-like mouths into the shark's flesh. Then their mouthparts begin scraping away. The mouthparts loosen bits of tissue for the copepods to feed on. This can cause infection in the shark. But only sharks that are sick or weak may die from these infections.

Parasites are not makos' biggest problem. Fishing is makos' greatest threat. Some fishing crews are small

Mako sharks are experiencing threats that are reducing their numbers in the ocean.

groups of people out sportfishing. Years ago, fishermen noticed what great fighters the makos were. The fishermen told stories about wild fishing trips. Makos, they said, were fast swimmers that leaped high in the air. They also praised the taste of shortfin meat. Word spread, and soon lots of people wanted to go mako fishing. Today, many makos are caught from sportfishing boats.

Sportfishing is not as big a threat as large-scale fishing is. Large-scale fishing crews roll out fishing lines in the ocean. The lines may be many miles long. The lines can have hundreds of hooks, each hook with bait. The fishing crews might be hoping for other fish, such as tuna. But makos grab the bait as well.

Other crews do fish for mako sharks. They know they can easily sell the sharks. Many restaurants serve mako dishes. One dish that is popular in several countries is shark fin soup. It is made with the fins of makos or other sharks. When fishing crews catch shortfin makos, they keep the sharks for their fins and meat.

Fishing is the main threat to mako sharks.

Fishing is reducing the number of mako sharks, but researchers are hoping to learn how to better protect their populations.

It is a different story for longfin makos. Crews know that longfin meat is not as tasty as shortfin meat. When the crews catch longfins, they often keep the fins but throw the bodies away.

Unfortunately, makos' popularity is causing problems. The number of makos around the world is shrinking. Both longfins and shortfins take years to grow up. Females do not have babies until they are almost 20 years old. Longfins might have only two babies at a time. It looks like the number of makos killed each year is higher than the number born each year. If this goes on, mako sharks will disappear.

Some shark experts are trying to solve this problem. There are now laws that limit shark fishing. However, these laws are hard to enforce. The United States and other countries ban fishermen bringing only shark fins to shore. Fishermen have to bring the bodies of sharks too. This prevents the wasteful practice of finning—taking the fins and throwing the rest of the shark back into the sea. However, this ban is not in place in all countries, and it is difficult to enforce.

Also, it is difficult to learn the true numbers of sharks caught every year. Experts don't know exactly how fast the sharks are disappearing. Researchers continue to study this problem in order to find a solution. They want mako sharks around for years to come.

THINK ABOUT IT

WHAT WERE THE SURPRISING FACTS YOU LEARNED FROM THIS CHAPTER? DISCUSS THESE WITH A FRIEND OR CLASSMATE.

THINK ABOUT IT

▲ Chapter 2 explained how a mako's countershading helps hide the animal. Why does the mako need to hide? Name some other animals whose colors help them hide.

▲ The longfin mako has larger eyes than the shortfin mako. Why do you think this is?

▲ In Chapter 4, you learned longfins and shortfins have different numbers of babies. Could the number of babies affect either of the shark populations' chances of survival? How?

▲ Read Chapter 5 again. What is the biggest threat facing mako sharks? Why is it so hard to put a stop to this threat? What could the public do to reduce the threat?

▲ What did you learn about mako sharks that surprised you?

LEARN MORE

BOOKS

Marsico, Katie. *Sharks*. New York: Scholastic, 2011.

Musgrave, Ruth. *Everything Sharks*. Washington, DC: National Geographic, 2011.

Smith, Miranda. *Sharks*. New York: Kingfisher, 2008.

WEB SITES

Discovery Kids—Sharks
http://kids.discovery.com/gaming/shark-week

This Web site lets readers play games and learn about shark attack survivals.

National Geographic—Sharks
http://animals.nationalgeographic.com/animals/sharks

Readers discover different species of sharks, learn more about the ocean, and play games at this Web site.

Shark Trust
http://www.sharktrust.org/juniors

On this Web site, readers can watch shark videos, play games, learn fun facts, and even adopt a shark.

GLOSSARY

apex (AY-pex) at the very top

cartilage (KAHR-tuh-lij) a hard, flexible tissue that forms certain parts of animals' bodies, such as a human ear or a shark's skeleton

cold-blooded (KOHLD BLUHD-id) having a body temperature that changes in relation to the temperature of its surroundings

countershading (KOUN-tur-shay-ding) the light and dark coloring of an animal to help it blend into its surroundings

mate (MATE) to join together to produce babies

parasite (PAR-uh-site) an organism that lives and feeds on another organism

pup (PUP) a baby shark

temperate (TEM-pur-it) not extremely hot or cold

warm-blooded (WAHRM BLUHD-id) having a body temperature that does not change, even if the surroundings are very hot or very cold

INDEX

body temperature, 17, 19

countershading, 11–12

gills, 10, 24

habitat, 7, 12
hunting, 4, 7, 14, 17, 19

laws, 28–29
longfin mako, 10–11, 12–13, 22, 28

mate, 20

physical features, 8–13, 22
prey, 4, 7, 8, 12, 14, 17, 19, 24
pups, 22–23

shortfin mako, 10–11, 12, 22, 26, 28
size, 12–13, 22, 23
speed, 4, 7, 8, 26

teeth, 10, 17
threats, human, 25–26, 28–29
threats, natural, 24–25